CU00902683

BOOK ANALYSIS

By Genevieve Zimantas

Wide Sargasso Sea

BY JEAN RHYS

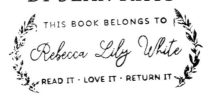

THIS BOOK BELONGS TO

Rebecca Lily White

READ IT · LOVE IT · RETURN IT

Bright
≡Summaries.com

JEAN RHYS

DOMINICAN NOVELIST AND SHORT STORY WRITER

- **Born in Roseau (Dominica) in 1890.**
- **Died in Exeter (United Kingdom) in 1979.**
- **Notable works:**
  - *Voyage in the Dark* (1934), novel
  - *Good Morning, Midnight* (1939), novel
  - *Sleep It Off Lady* (1976), short story collection

Born to a Welsh doctor and his white Creole wife in Dominica, British West Indies, Jean Rhys spent her childhood in a world defined by change as colonial and race relations shifted and intensified around her. Following her father's death, Rhys moved to England to attend an all-girls school. She had trouble fitting in with her British peers, however, and soon left to become a chorus girl and dancer. Married three times, Rhys's adult life was defined by heartache and instability. She turned her hand to writing early but did not publish any of her work until she met the English writer Ford Maddox Ford (1873-1939) while her first husband, Jean Lenglet, was in prison. She then published four short novels and a collection of stories in the 1920s and 1930s before experiencing a period of slow production following the start of the Second World War. She published *Wide Sargasso Sea* in 1966. The novel won her international recognition and is now considered her masterpiece.

WIDE SARGASSO SEA

RESPONDING TO *JANE EYRE* (1847) IN FICTION

- **Genre:** novel
- **Reference edition:** Rhys, J. (1966) Wide Sargasso Sea. In: D. Athill, ed. (1985) *The Complete Novels*. New York: W. W. Norton & Co., pp. 463-574.
- **1st edition:** 1966
- **Themes:** race, colonialism, gender, marriage, love, desire, power, manipulation

Wide Sargasso Sea was written while Rhys was experiencing a period of ill health and isolation, and returns to the universe of Charlotte Brontë's *Jane Eyre* (1847) to tell a different story: that of the character Brontë called Bertha Mason, the "madwoman in the attic". Renaming the "madwoman" Antoinette, *Wide Sargasso Sea* follows its protagonist through an ideologically confusing childhood as the daughter of a former slave owner in a world on the brink of change. It then continues to follow her through her first encounters with the unnamed Rochester figure, through their marriage and initial period of lustful happiness, and into the turmoil of dishonesty and suspicion which poisons their marriage and steers her life towards its tragic end.

Generally accepted as one of the singular masterpieces of 20th-century fiction, Rhys's final novel predates the field of postcolonial studies by nearly twenty years and gave rise to a whole series of novels which similarly "write back" *to* or *against* major canonical works from the Victorian period.

SUMMARY

PART ONE: A COMPLICATED CHILDHOOD

Recalling the events of her childhood at the very beginning of *Wide Sargasso Sea*, Antoinette Bertha Mason, née Cosway, introduces both the complex race relations and the feelings of alienation which define much of her life: "They say when trouble comes close ranks, and so the white people did. But we were not among their ranks" (p. 465). Detailing memories of the family horse being killed and of a young black playmate, the daughter of slaves, stealing her clothes after swimming, Antoinette contextualizes her first statement in a general sense of unease. Her family is white, but not a part of the white community. Neither are they black or part of any other local community. These unnamed tensions do not come to a head, however, until a group of former slaves burns down the family estate in the dead of night, killing Antoinette's infant brother, Pierre, driving her mother into madness, and leaving Antoinette in the care of her step-father, Richard Mason.

In accordance with her step-father's wishes, Antoinette goes to live with her Aunt Cora and attend the Mount Calvary Convent in Spanish Town, Jamaica. She enjoys the convent, calling it her "refuge" (p. 490), but also admits that she felt "bolder, happier, more free. But not so safe" (p. 492).

Richard Mason visits her often while she is at the convent but does not bring up the question of marriage until his final visit, when he talks about bringing an English friend to see her. Antoinette is consumed by "a feeling of dismay, sadness, loss" (p. 493). She dreams she is wearing a long white dress and being led through the dark by a sinister stranger. "I dreamed I was in Hell," she says (*ibid.*).

PART TWO: TWO VOICES

Both Antoinette and her new husband (who is never named in the novel) act as narrators in Part Two of *Wide Sargasso Sea*, with the Rochester fi-gure's narration of their married life bookending

Antoinette's section in the middle. His narration begins in a cynical tone which seems to reinforce Antoinette's dread from the end of Part One and to undermine any lingering sense of hope Rhys's protagonist held: "So it was all over," he writes, "everything finished, for better or for worse" (p. 495). And then, later, "I played the part I was expected to play" but "it meant nothing to me. Nor did she, the girl I was to marry" (p. 502). Rhys does not describe the wedding itself; instead, she includes a flashback scene in which Antoinette tries to refuse her future husband's proposal. When pressed further, Antoinette justifies her attempted refusal by saying "I'm afraid of what may happen" (p. 504), but her suitor eventually convinces her: "'I'll trust you if you'll trust me. Is that a bargain?' [...] She did not answer me. Only nodded" (*ibid.*).

The couple travel through Jamaica to reach the family property at Granbois, with Antoinette's husband recovering from a severe fever. Their married life begins there. Fuelled by lust and what he perceives as the beautiful exoticism of his new wife and their surroundings, Antoinette and her husband settle into an uneasy kind of happiness.

However, this happiness does not last long and a letter soon arrives from a supposed relative named Daniel Cosway, besmirching Antoinette's character by insinuating that she is both mad and unchaste. Rhys's male narrator initially brushes the letter off, but the accusations sink into his subconscious. Hoping to restore their married bliss, Antoinette goes to Christophine, her childhood nurse and a practitioner of Obeah (a Voodoo-like religion originating in the Caribbean), for a love potion. Her husband becomes convinced that she is trying to poison him. He grows cruel and decides to take Antoinette away to England without consulting her.

PART THREE: UP IN FLAMES

Antoinette is the sole narrator of Part Three, in which she is held prisoner in her bedroom in the Rochester figure's English home and guarded there by a servant named Grace Poole. Suspended in a kind of dream state, she reflects on her situation:

> "When I first came I thought it would be for a day, two days, a week perhaps. I thought that when I saw him and spoke to him I would be wise

as serpents, harmless as doves. 'I give you all I have freely,' I would say, 'and I will not trouble you again if you will let me go.' But he never came." (p. 567)

Becoming increasingly desperate, Antoinette begins to focus on fire as a way to warm herself against the country in which she finds herself, which seems cold to her in both Brontë's novel and her own story. Foreshadowing the end of Brontë's novel in her own, Antoinette has a recurring dream about escaping her room and freeing herself with fire and then fleeing "the heat and the shouting" (p. 574) by jumping into the open air. She brings her narrative full circle by imagining her childhood playmate in a seemingly prophetic vision of her own end: "All this I saw and heard in a fraction of a second. And the sky so red. Someone screamed and I thought, *Why did I scream?* I called 'Tia!' and jumped and woke" (*ibid.*)

CHARACTER STUDY

ANTOINETTE COSWAY

Antoinette Bertha Mason, née Cosway, is the white Creole daughter of a former slave owner and his wife. A timid child, she has complex feelings about her position as a member of the white ruling class in 19th-century Jamaica but is unable to see the extent of her privilege. Feeling excluded by both the white and black communities around her family, she even envies the sense of belonging she perceives among her black peers: "They hated us. They called us white cockroaches" (p. 469) she says before recounting a story of a girl her own age following her and singing "Go away white cockroach, go away, go away" (*ibid.*).

Antoinette is described as a beautiful woman with long dark hair which falls "smoothly far below her waist" (p. 504) and eyes her husband describes as "too large and [...] disconcerting. [...] Long, sad, dark alien eyes" (p. 496).

ANTOINETTE'S HUSBAND (THE UNNAMED ROCHESTER FIGURE)

The male protagonist in Rhys's novel is never named and, though clearly meant to represent the same person as Brontë's hero, has not yet become the Rochester Brontë's readers know so well. Here identified as a second son who stands to inherit neither money nor property from his father, the Rochester figure in Rhys's novel gets his money and power from marriage—in other words, from the dowry Antoinette brings with her from her step-father.

He is fickle and allows himself to be manipulated into turning against Antoinette even though he had previously promised to protect and trust her.

His physical features are almost never described, except for one passage in which he jokes about a frangipani wreath not suiting his "handsome face" (p. 500). Antoinette responds, "You look like a king, an emperor" (*ibid.*), symbolically placing her husband in the role of the colonial ruler in their marriage.

CHRISTOPHINE

Christophine is a woman from Martinique whom Antoinette introduces to her husband as "my da, my nurse long ago" (p. 499), and who had been her mother's slave, a wedding gift from her marriage to Antoinette's father.

Antoinette says of Christophine that "Her songs were not like Jamaican songs, and she was not like the other women. She was much blacker – blue-black with a thin face and straight features. She wore a black dress, heavy gold earrings and a yellow handkerchief – carefully tied with two high points in front." (p. 467).

A practitioner of Obeah, Christophine is generally feared and respected by the other members of their community. She unsettles Antoinette's husband.

ANNETTE

Antoinette's mother is described as an extraordinarily beautiful woman and a wonderful dancer. Twice married, she is fiercely defensive of her sickly infant son and leaves Antoinette feeling somewhat overlooked as a result. After the destruction of their home and Pierre's death she tries to harm herself, Antoinette, and her husband Richard Mason. She is taken away and dies soon afterwards.

PIERRE

Pierre is Antoinette's sickly infant brother whom Daniel Cosway describes as "an idiot from birth" (p. 506). Conscious of his fragility, Antoinette writes that he sleeps in a crib long after he should have grown out of one and "was so thin that I could lift him easily" (p. 478).

AUNT CORA

Described by Antoinette as "an ex-slave owner who had escaped misery" (p. 473), Aunt Cora is the widow of an English gentleman who moved back to Jamaica to live in Spanish Town after his death. Resilient and practical, she stands up to the black crowd which gathers after the family home burns down in Part One, protesting their need to get Pierre to a doctor. Antoinette describes her as smelling "of vanilla" (p. 479).

RICHARD MASON

"A very wealthy man" (p. 472), Antoinette's stepfather is naïve about the severity of racial tensions at the beginning of the novel and ignores his wife's pleas that they move elsewhere.

Antoinette describes him fondly but also specifies that she "still called him 'Mr Mason' in my head. 'Goodnight white pappy,' I said one evening and he was not vexed, he laughed" (p. 476).

TIA

Tia is the black daughter of a friend of Christophine's, and is Antoinette's only childhood friend. Antoinette describes her with awe, stating that "fires always lit for her, sharp stones did not hurt her bare feet, I never saw her cry" (p. 469).

However, Tia is more cognizant of the racial divide between them and has a more complicated opinion of Antoinette, which ultimately leads her to strike her with a stone on the night of the fire.

DANIEL COSWAY

Describing himself as Antoinette's *"brother by another lady"* (p. 515), Daniel Cosway is partially based on the Shakespearean character of Iago. He sends Antoinette's husband the letter besmirching her character and plants seeds of doubt in his mind regarding her chastity and sanity.

ANALYSIS

ANSWERING THE MARRIAGE PLOT

Wide Sargasso Sea features a marriage plot (a common narrative structure in the Victorian era which now thrives in the cinematic genre of the romantic comedy) but it breaks the usual mould by telling the story of a failed marriage. It is particularly interesting to consider this narrative element in the light of the work that inspired *Wide Sargasso Sea*: namely, *Jane Eyre* by Charlotte Brontë (British writer, 1816-1855).

"I admire her greatly" (*Letters, 1931-66* (1985): p. 175), Rhys once wrote to a friend about Charlotte Brontë, and, speaking also of Brontë's sister Emily (British writer, 1818-1848), elaborated, "I envy them both more than I can say" (*ibid.*). Upon first reading *Jane Eyre* as a teenager growing up in Dominica, Rhys loved the world of romance and fulfillment detailed in Charlotte Brontë's famous Victorian novel, but she also lamented the role of the character with whom she most closely identified. Bertha Mason is a character Rhys felt was "not once alive" (*Letters, 1931-66* (1985): p. 156) in the original novel. She is Rochester's wife, but because of her supposed "madness" and her status as an outsider—because she is of Creole descent, non-English and therefore "other"—she functions more as an obstacle to be overcome by the protagonist than as a character in her own right. As Rhys wrote decades later in a letter to her editor, Diana Athill, "She's necessary to the plot, but always shrieks, howls, laughs horribly, attacks all and sundry—*off stage*" (*Letters, 1931-66* (1985): *ibid.*). Part of Rhys's reasoning for writing her version of the story was to bring that marginalized character *on* stage and to let her tell "*her* story" (*Letters, 1931-66* (1985): p. 157), revealing a new side of the story we all know.

In writing her own version of Brontë's character, Rhys therefore faced a clear narrative dilemma: how to write the story of a character whose fate has already been decided by another novelist, who has decreed that she will go mad and burn her husband's house to the ground with people still inside it. Rhys solves this problem by taking the reader back to Antoinette's childhood and telling the story of a different marriage plot: not Jane's but Bertha's own. By telling Antoinette's story from the beginning, Rhys's novel also proves that it is less interested in "what" happened to make Bertha burn Rochester's house down than in "why" she did. *Wide Sargasso Sea*'s aim is to tell a story that explains why Bertha developed this particular type of madness, and why she became so desperate that she was willing to harm herself and others in order to escape her own reality.

POWER AND BELONGING

Questions of power and of belonging dominate Rhys's novel. When Antoinette writes at the very beginning of *Wide Sargasso Sea* that "They say when trouble comes close ranks, and so the white people did. But we were not among their ranks" (p. 465), she is not only alluding to the social circumstances which made her family vulnerable to the attack that cost them their home and killed her infant brother, but also the psychological circumstances in which she grew up.

From the very beginning of the novel, belonging is shown to be important to Antoinette, who does not feel like she is accepted by either the white or black populations around her and is spurned by Tia, her only childhood friend. This un-belonging also leaves her vulnerable to manipulation and, ultimately, to psychological abuse and imprisonment. With no real family to care for her after her mother goes mad and her step-father marries her off, there is no one left to protect her. Rochester decides that she is insane and decides to hide her away in a country that is foreign to her.

THE DIFFERENCE BETWEEN LOVE AND LUST

One of the more radical arguments *Wide Sargasso Sea* makes about the relationship between Antoinette and her husband centres on the sexual relationship between the two characters. At first, Rochester seems pleased that "very soon she was as eager for what's called loving as I was – more lost and drowned afterwards" (p. 513). However, he soon comes to see her eagerness as part of her madness and moral failing.

Where Antoinette continues to associate their love-making with falling in love, he soon comes to hate her for it and to use her lust for him to justify his false opinions about her.

PLOTTING A TRAGEDY

In addition to Brontë's *Jane Eyre*, Rhys wrote *Wide Sargasso Sea* partly in reaction to Shakespeare's *Othello* (1603). As Rhys once wrote, describing her hero in terms of both Shakespeare's great tragedy and Emily Brontë's hero in *Wuthering Heights* (1959), he is "as fierce as Heathcliff and as jealous as Othello..." (qtd. in Stoneman (1996): p. 181).

Othello tells the story of a Moorish general in the Venetian army whose treacherous ensign, Iago, poisons his happy marriage by suggesting that Othello's wife, Desdemona, has been unfaithful to him. In Shakespeare's version of the story, Othello ends up killing Desdemona before committing suicide himself.

The unnamed Rochester figure does not kill Antoinette in *Wide Sargasso Sea*, but the influence of Shakespeare's drama is nonetheless clear: like Iago in *Othello*, Daniel Cosway plants suspicion in the hero's mind, and like Othello himself, Antoinette's husband allows that suspicion to dictate his actions. He may not kill Antoinette directly, but he does withhold his love and lock her up away from everything and everyone she has ever known, driving her into the very madness of which he accuses her in both *Jane Eyre* and *Wide Sargasso Sea*, which eventually leads to her death.

WHAT'S IN A NAME?

Wide Sargasso Sea is clearly a response to *Jane Eyre*, and makes many references which tie its fictional universe directly to that of Brontë's novel. Richard Mason retains his role as familial guardian; Grace Poole also keeps her name and her role from the earlier novel; even Antoinette's madness is, by the end, uncontested. But Rhys also makes some deliberate and meaningful changes which re-contextualize the earlier novel rather than refuting it.

Names are a prominent way in which she "writes back" against her literary predecessor, refusing to name her hero and renaming his bride Antoinette. Brontë's original name for the "madwoman" does feature in Rhys's novel, but as a kind of game and source of tension: "will you come in and say goodnight to me?" (p. 541) Antoinette asks her husband as he begins to succumb to hatred and suspicion. "Certainly I will, my dear Bertha" (*ibid.*) he answers. Antoinette protests that she does not want to be called Bertha but ultimately submits to the name. "Of course, on this night of all nights, you must be Bertha," he tells her (*ibid.*). In this way, he forces her into the role the earlier novel fated her to play.

EVERYTHING ON FIRE

Fire functions as a fundamental symbol in Rhys's novel which ties her fiction to Brontë's while also holding her own novel together and representing her heroine's unavoidable fate.

Significantly, the novel both begins and ends with fire. At the beginning of the novel, Antoinette's childhood home burns down and her mother's parrot, Coco, comes flying out of the building on fire—a local sign of bad luck. This first fire kills her brother and causes her mother to go mad. The second fire only features in a dream in Rhys's novel but concretely foreshadows the real fire which kills Bertha Mason in *Jane Eyre*. It is the crystallization of her madness and the solution which frees Rochester from his marriage to her, thereby allowing him to marry Jane and complete his second, happier marriage plot.

FURTHER REFLECTION

SOME QUESTIONS TO THINK ABOUT...

- Given the importance of names in Rhys's novel, why does Antoinette's husband remain nameless?
- It could be said that Antoinette has three mother figures in this novel: Annette, Aunt Cora, and Christophine. How do these mother figures differ? Do they each shape Antoinette's character?
- Dreams and magic play an important role in *Wide Sargasso Sea*. How does Christophine's wisdom and her use of Obeah compare to the Rochester figure's rationality and colonial power?
- Antoinette is the daughter of a former slave owner and yet envies her childhood friend Tia. What do you make of this perception of reality? What does Antoinette understand and fail to understand about the world around her?
- Rhys' characters frequently take up the

language of Brontë's hero to call Antoinette "Intemperate and unchaste" (Brontë, 2004: p. 397). What other linguistic or symbolic parallels can you find between the two novels? What is the significance of this mimicking?

- How does the inclusion of both Antoinette and her husband as first-person narrators impact our reading of the novel? How much can we trust or not trust what characters like Antoinette and her husband say about themselves or each other?

- What is the true significance of madness in this novel? What might cause a person in Rhys's novel to go mad?

We want to hear from you!
Leave a comment on your online library
and share your favourite books on social media!

FURTHER READING

REFERENCE EDITION

- Rhys, J. (1966) Wide Sargasso Sea. In: D. Athill, ed. (1985) *The Complete Novels*. New York: W. W. Norton & Co., pp. 463-574.

REFERENCE STUDIES

- Brontë, C. (2004) *Jane Eyre*. Peterborough: Broadview Press Ltd.

- Rhys, J. (1985) *Letters, 1931-66*. Ed. F. Wyndham and D. Melly. Middlesex: Penguin Books Ltd.

- Stoneman, P. (1996) *Brontë Transformations: The Cultural Dissemination of* Jane Eyre *and* Wuthering Heights. Cornwall: Hartnolls Ltd.

ADDITIONAL SOURCES

- Kaplan, C. (2007) *Victoriana: Histories, Fictions, Criticisms*. New York: Columbia University Press.

- Savory, E. (1998) *Cambridge Studies in African and Caribbean Literature: Jean Rhys*. Cambridge: Cambridge University Press.

ADAPTATIONS

- *Wide Sargasso Sea*. (1993) [Film]. John Duigan. Dir. USA: Fine Line Features.

- *Wide Sargasso Sea*. (2006) [Television Miniseries]. Brendan Maher. Dir. UK: BBC Wales, Kudos Film and Television.

MORE FROM BRIGHTSUMMARIES.COM

- Reading guide – *Jane Eyre* by Charlotte Brontë.

www.brightsummaries.com

Ebook EAN: 9782808012263

Paperback EAN: 9782808012270

Legal Deposit: D/2018/12603/362

Cover: © Primento

Digital conception by Primento, the digital partner of
publishers.